THE WORLD RETURNING

LAWRENCE SAIL

The World Returning

BLOODAXE BOOKS

ISBN: 1 85224 591 3

First published 2002 by
Bloodaxe Books Ltd,
Highgreen,
Tarset,
Northumberland NE48 1RP.

www.bloodaxebooks.com
For further information about Bloodaxe titles
please visit our website or write to
the above address for a catalogue.

Bloodaxe Books Ltd acknowledges
the financial assistance of Northern Arts.

Cover printing by J. Thomson Colour Printers Ltd, Glasgow.

Printed in Great Britain by
Cromwell Press Ltd, Trowbridge, Wiltshire.

for Jimmy and Margie Campbell

Acknowledgements

Acknowledgements are due to the editors of the following publications in which some of these poems first appeared: *The Arvon Journal, Critical Survey, Leviathan Quarterly, Mosaic* (Penguin Books/ British Council, 1998), *New Writing 10* (Picador / The British Council, 2001), *Oxford Magazine, Pitch, PN Review, Poetry Ireland Review, Poetry Kanto, Poetry Review, The Rialto* and *Stand*.

The sequence 'Six Songs' was commissioned for the opening of the Layard Theatre at Canford School, and set to music by Isabelle Ryder.

Lawrence Sail also gratefully acknowledges support for the writing of 'Out of Silence', the settings of the poems by Isabelle Ryder and their performance in a series of concerts, from the Poetry Society, The Year of the Artist/South West Arts, Exeter Arts Council and the Arts Council of England.

Contents

Theatre Opening

Men must know, that in this theatre of man's life
it is reserved only for God and angels to be lookers on
FRANCIS BACON,
'Advancement of Learning'

This is the reservoir flooded to full
for the first time. It flows and wells,
its surface a restless glitter, its depths
already an unsounded spell.

This is the warehouse of ghosts which hoards
the poisoner's whispers, doomed queens and kings,
tramps in waiting and, beyond the wood
at Colonus, Œdipus fading.

This is where vowels imagine everything –
that wooden O, Poseidon's E,
upturned steel U, aluminium A,
I on a headland by the sea.

For this is state of the art darkness
in which the mind, all synaptic relays,
knows itself warded by true pretence,
a play within a play.

Everything here is absorbed on cue –
the belly laugh, the lethal kiss,
the armed silence, the unguarded look:
there is no end to this.

So begin. Bring on the hopeful lovers
with their young gestures, and the kindly clowns.
Here, as outside, only God and his angels
may claim to be lookers on.

1

Gas-masks

They seem to express compassion of a kind
with their goggling eyes and round snouts;
and strangeness, like Van Helmont's made-up word
for the stuff itself, with its little hiss of pressure.

As I child I found one, discarded in a cellar,
the prize item in a trove of junk:
its pepperpot perforations gave a glimpse
of electric blue, its rubber trachea jiggled.

Gas – which threatened to make the dentist's
more sinister still, which burned at a beak
like a blue butterfly, which could bloom in astonishing
whiteness in the fragile cotton mantle of the lamp.

I tried on the mask, a juju talisman
that promoted my breath to a loud rasp,
projected the world as two scratchy circles,
enclosed my head in a band of clumsy tightness.

Soldiers, I knew, came into it – and rattles,
and men with bandaged eyes, each
with a hand on the shoulder of the man in front,
groping forward through the bright day in darkness.

That night I dreamt of gas-masked figures
swathed and helmeted, visible only
now and then, as they walked calmly
through bluffs of drifting smoke in the wake of a battle.

Alien beadsmen, they nodded their way
among the dead, saying nothing,
their shiny eyepieces utterly blank,
as if they knew the worst was yet to come.

The Pilots' Tea Dance

Everything at a slant:
the diagonal shiny boards,
the spotlight's smoky shaft,
the way they move the girls
held in their chevroned arms
to the sly foxtrot, the waltz;
and the camera that peers down
as if in search of hindsight.

Out of the sun, they wave
like the summer wheat outside,
lost in the only dream
that could hope to out-sing time
or the voice which knows that the field
is the world, and the reapers, angels.

The Musical Box
(for Catriona)

In the dark space under the basement stairs, it seemed
too big to be a casket. A child's coffin,
we sometimes thought, although it weighed a ton.
Never polished, it always gleamed and gleamed.

We hardly noticed, inside the lid, the display
of almost naked nymphs whose gauzy veils
wafted so decently. There were too many other things,
beneath an inner glass lid, to claim our attention:
the great rolling cylinder pimpled with tunes,
the double row of chimes and the strikers, each
stem topped with a little turban of brass;
the rabbit's ear of the lever which brought the strikers
to the bells or away; the great comb of metal
on which the music played. Best of all, the vane
that pirouetted on its spindle, its little paddles
easy to put a finger in and stop,
then let go again. Not to mention the tunes themselves,
twelve of them, every one prinked and decorated
with ornate arpeggios, *glissandi* bright as rain –
Can-can, Strauss, the Russian anthem, Brahms.

Squeezed in beside the box, sister and brother,
we might have been back in the womb – ghostly twins
hardly hearing the world, any more than the beat
of the flicking vane. Hardly knowing each other.

Painting of an Island

I dream of the prow with a bone in its teeth
and the foam squirting in two Welsh plumes,
the hull lifting, quivering like a fish,
falling with the thud of truth.

And astern, dwindling till it hardly rides
the swell, the mainland: ahead, somewhere,
the island hidden by the endless shimmers
that cross the muscle of the tide.

It lies just over the strait. On Sundays
surely you could hear the bells, the prayers,
our Father – or laughter, from the houses
with verandahs and a view of the bay.

I know where it comes from, this little franchise
of biscuit-flat land crammed between towers,
with its church in a hidden square to which
the hidden streets must rise.

And I know how those two open boats on the quay,
one careened like an Auden slipper,
will always suggest the ease of crossing
and how it will always be

as out of reach, that island, as the parent
who sent his paintings for the children's rooms –
whose memory, over the years, became
ruinous with absence.

Black in the Early 1950s

For a start, the bags under Edgar Lustgarten's eyes
as he shook his jowls morosely towards the stalls
from his leather chair, a coal fire licking behind him –
Of all the cases that baffled Scotland Yard
surely none was more strange than that of the headless
body at Midhurst Station, one bleak winter night...

And then the film itself, in which an ambulance,
black, top-heavy, with great silver hinges,
would career down the curvy drive of a private clinic
in which some unspeakable procedure would be performed
without anaesthetic. Only the imagination,
wincing, could get past the doors with their blind port-holes.

In real life, it could be just as bad – a man
wrapped in red blankets and held in place with straps,
carried from a house in the street. Not a good colour.
The ambulance gleaming like a hearse, the silver trolley
shiny as a fish. We children gawped. They slid him
in on runners and shut him into the dark.

Back at the clinic, at the very moment when
the eyes above the mask narrowed, pitiless, and the hand
moved to make the incision, more sugar-crunching
of wheels on gravel – enter two black Wolseleys
with alarms clanging, rocking on their springs as out
leapt squads of policemen, all in their smartest black.

In 1952, a month or so before Newcastle
won the Cup for the second year running, black went
ballistic. Even the wireless rigged up at school
had its square face wimpled in black cotton
for The Funeral. Voices were solemn, close to tears.
One boy fainted. The teachers wore black ties.

Looking back, though, it's clear that really nothing
we saw at the Gaumont, the Odeon or the Savoy,
or in the street, or heard on the wireless at school
could hope to outdo the black of the late forties –
the aftermath of war, the cat slinking
across the dazzling dark toecaps of Harry Lime's shoes.

The Addiction

All this came late, as seemed to befit a house
with no father, where taboos had a low threshold –
you could make do with a sniff at an empty beer-bottle,
a lick of its black nubbed stopper; or with a quick
glimpse of the pub when the frosted door swung open,
the waft of talk and smoke yeastily there
and gone again. Once, a bottle of rum
with a top you flipped up, and the strange smell of dunder.

The litany of brands could well have been
a sufficient lure – Craven 'A', Abdullah,
Woodbines, Capstan Full Strength, Senior Service,
Player's Navy Cut, Du Maurier, Three Castles,
Gold Flake, Gitanes, Gold Leaf, even the absurd
exotic Balkan Sobranies with their gold-tipped black,
and the ones in soft packs closed with a paper seal:
Lucky Strike, Disques Bleus, Camels, Chesterfield.

Then, the procedures: the opening of the little drawer,
the whoosh, soft as satin, when you whisked away
the gold or silver foil, to expose them ranged
in perfect order, close and regular
as boxed eggs. Or, breaking the seal,
you gave that one authoritative tap
which brought out two or three just so far,
stacked like organ pipes, ready to offer.

After that, timing and expression were everything:
the flick of fire, the head inclined and then
tossed back, the lips and cheeks closed in on
the searing circle, the arc of the hand, the cool
considered exhalation and the look
that went with it. Whole systems could be stubbed
out, arguments clinched, an ache in the heart
be noble, or a hot affair be started.

It took another twenty years to learn
that real addiction might be something else –
the world returning, hyper-real enough
to drag your eyes from their sockets, and the size
of every leaf outsize, each object swollen
with its own savour and abundance. Even to enjoy,
when it was safe, the whiff of cedar and, slightly,
of caporal in the box with no cigarettes.

In Outline Only

As for the bedroom walls, three were already
full – the good old Kodak always did
the trick. Amazing, how at that age they loved
to pose. He focused them upright or horizontal
in the viewfinder's shining cross, flirtatious creatures!
Still room for more, though: the possibilities seemed endless.

*

Here was another twelve year old (or was he
only eleven then?) laughing, sucking on a pipe:
and there, a boy standing up through the sun-roof, waving.
Happy days. In this one, someone was trying
to light a fire outside a two-man tent.

*

He gave them presents and meant them. He also liked
the feel of flesh – to deliver a hard smack
and then let his hand stay clamped to the buttocks.
He regularly felt the need to pray.

*

He teased them with things they could not possibly know,
though he himself was puzzled by the way
in which one friendship ended, and another
soon began. They just did, it seemed.

*

As for the bedroom, impossible to tell
which of the pics were trophies, which (if any)
temptation withstood – and whether it was guilt
or simple prudence which made him strip the walls
bare one day, get rid of everything.

*

His later holidays were spent discreetly
in Bangkok or the Philippines. At home,
something that was not love but knew its gestures
ghosted the paler patches on the walls –
in outline only mirroring the stain
of hard facts spreading out through all those lives.

Pointing to Persia

In Figure 78, England is supposed
to be at the top of the globe. Look
at the boy in Figure 79:
his shorts come neatly down to his knees,
his socks are pulled right up to them also.
His perfectly straight left arm extends
to his index finger, which in turn jabs
at four o'clock. This boy is pointing to Persia.

That boy is leaving his teethmarks embedded
in his pencil, and shifting on his shiny seat:
the world is all before him, its outlines
have been rolled off a cylinder onto paper.
He has ten minutes in which to trace
the course of the Orinoco, and to show
the wheat-growing areas of Manitoba
and Winnipeg, to mark in Hobart, and the Friendly Isles.

Homework will be the Dogger Bank,
where the low black trawlers drag their nets
off coastlines blanket-stitched in blue.
Later, other subjects will produce
their own maps: mark the position of the lungs,
the kidneys. You see? A perfect system
of pink obedience. And now, everyone
point to Bombay; to the Nile; to the Torrid Zone.

Fives Courts
(for Matthew)

In every place the courts were set apart,
hidden behind the armoury or the bike sheds,
a good place for a quick grope or a gasper.
Empty, they seemed banal as a torturer's cellar:
a row of sties that didn't smell quite right.

Blank walls, a toy door, four large lights
in metal shades with grilles, shining onto
slabbed stone. Along the front, a bar
of wood. In autumn, the courts streamed with wet:
in winter, the wind drove snow across the thresholds.

In an old biscuit tin, a selection of gloves
limp as exhausted fish; Slazengers, the colour
of dried blood, Grasshoppers a dull grey.
In most, the fingers unstitched, the padding lumpy:
in all, an ingrained smell of stale sweat.

Only the ball was intricate. On old ones,
like mad surgery, little spiralling lines
of red stitches pulled the cover tight
around a core of rubber, cotton and cork.
Nowadays they just glue the seams into place.

The play's the thing, pure ingenuity –
the crack of a service rocketing out from the corner,
the ball hammered off the back wall, the sly lob,
the boast that ricochets madly off one or both
side-walls and dies irretrievably by the bar.

Enter the ghost of Hazlitt, himself a player,
who wrote that 'poetry puts a spirit of life
and motion into the universe' – and knew
how much depended on the playful imagination,
on keeping warm in the coldest places on earth.

Not Admitting It

Your world worked almost perfectly: in your cellar
the beer ticked and fizzed. On your allotment,
year after year the scarlet beans raced up
the crossed poles, onions swelled their copper domes,
raspberries delivered their soft drupels by the score.

You had the world's number, knew to avoid
redcaps, rozzers, all agents of the state.
During the war, you heated your steak and kidney
on a tank engine's cover. In peacetime, drove too fast
(your wife knitting like fury) but spotted all speed traps.

Perfectly at ease, you went about trailing
a tea-cloth and duster, one from each trouser pocket.
Your moustache came and went – the pipe as well,
which took its turn with hand-rolled Rizlas so thin
they almost went up in the lighter's flame completely.

Confident, too – God knows what you smuggled out,
wrapped in brown paper, from the college buttery, certain
that somebody's blind eye was turned. And proud of your fitness,
bracing your stomach muscles, then inviting
a punch: *Go on, have another go! Harder!*

Your stories, like your laughter, described a place
in which, if you kept your wits, and one step ahead,
anything was possible. Scouting the world as it was,
you tutored us to share your love of jokes,
to see that defeat was the biggest joke of all.

Even at the end, when you lay all huddled up
in a hospital bed, you couldn't admit it, but just
yawned hugely, your tongue wagging mute in the middle.
All I could do was say *Take it easy, George*
and turn away: I knew you had gone already.

For Tony Lambert

Last night, hearing of your death at fifty-two,
I scanned the college photo of sixty-three,
willing you not to be there, among the rows
of the peaked-too-soon, the yet-to-become, the just right
pipe-smoking Tories, brilliant historians,
inscrutable civil servants of the future,
union officials, doctors, publishers, priests –
there, reliably, you weren't. And perhaps it is
that consistency of absence which makes it now
not just simple, but an imperative
to run to words so soon, somehow to track
that real and timeless ground which lies beyond
the real immediacies of grief and anger.

For time was never in it, not even in
the pendulum of the weighty gray and yellow
iron pan you gave me for my wedding,
though thirty years on it still makes wicked omelettes.
Somewhere I have a picture of you holding it,
in the front quad, on the day. Your smile. Your wide
eyes, a little heavy. Your relaxed stance –
everything conveying the flair I loved
and feared a little, because it seemed to offer
no guarantee of anything but itself,
and sometimes came too close to undermining
that notional justice which, I naively hoped,
might somehow still secure the world ahead.

Somewhere. Sometimes. Somehow. More recently,
we talked of meeting again, although our voices
down the line could hardly disturb the old
continuity of silence. And now, only this
monologue – but held clear of circumstance,
in a way that I think you would find funny, but also
understand. Your last plans, I hear,
included poems and an art gallery. I can offer
no other presence than this, along with the image
which I found today, on waking, in my head –
of a burnished fruit turning calmly on its branch:
perfect, beyond the reach of any trespass,
remote as the moon and radical as love.

Cutting the Bay Hedge

Each year it takes me half a day
to cut the fifteen-foot high bay
hedge at the front, and each year
it seems to shoot up taller earlier.
Steps are required, shears, a long
pole with a blade that cuts down one
limb at a time. From the hedge's summit
bees and butterflies burst out of it.

This summer again I stand shakily
up in mid-air, hoping not to make
myself unbalance by sneezing at the scent –
heady, a bit peppery, pungent –
of the glossy leaves: and peer by chance
skywards to where the topmost branches
wave in dark silhouette, distressed
by the breeze, blocking the sun's brightness.

And there is Victory, complete with wings
as she featured in my childhood, presiding
high on the war memorial, in the gardens
opposite the gaol. Below her, each warding
a compass point, a sailor astride
a broken boat, a soldier supplied
with full kit, a nurse in boots,
a prisoner with chains snapped, boldly resolute.

Victory herself stood four square
on a splayed dragon which just lay there
with jaws open, still eager to snap –
subdued, but biding its time perhaps,
its tail curling off the edge of the plinth.
Victory stood her ground, unflinching:
in her left hand a sword, unsheathed,
her right waving a laurel wreath.

But none of this was like the war
we children knew from films we saw –
our minds were flooded with U-boats gliding

through cloudy depths, POWs hiding
in wooden horses, bombs that bounced,
Spitfires, Messerschmitts, Tommies trouncing
blockheaded Nazis who screamed and swore,
their panzers knocked out on the long shore.

And at the Odeon on Saturdays
close to the bombsites where we played,
in the interval slowly they led on
the blind pianist who played songs
so that we could make the miles fewer
to the sweetest Tipperary girl we knew,
or pack up our troubles in our fathers' style
using old kitbags and a three-part smile.

Anyway, all that was long before
I had the dreams in which I saw
the green hill and the red blood,
or stared with a disbelieving shudder
at the skull in the museum case
hoopla-ed with a lopsided crown, its face
a mockery. Before I knew
the nightmare histories to be true.

The pole tests its weight against mine:
hooking a branch, I pull on the line
and a sprig with green berries tumbles to the ground.
Cut by cut I work down
to the spider-kingdom of branch and root,
the endless ply and involution
of tough, inveterate growth, the dark
and sooty wood with its pale heart.

The cut hedge curves against the sky.
I fold the steps from A to I,
sweep and bag the clippings, aching
but satisfied – finding only later
bay-leaves neat as visiting cards
filed in my pocket as they fell earthwards:
less souvenirs than indices
of the oncoming past, still unappeased.

2

Winter Solstice

This is the light least known,
not flashily occulting
or fixed in the sea, steady,
but a deep fire hiding
like a peaty secret sown
at the core of a heath, ready
to burn for as many years
as it takes, the friable ash
collapsing like calcined bone.
This is the true moth-light
by which the eye perceives
the dark dazzle of the earth:
by which the heart believes
it is warmed and not consumed.

Sky-blue

It is a deceit, the sky-blue sea,
and means no good. Pent in its slopes
the lost ship heels hard over, its jib
a flyaway hope, the starboard gunwale
scoured in rushing salt.

There is no compass by which to steer
safe through the steep brunt of the waves;
no light to fix on, no hand to steady
the crazy wheel, no nail or caulking
secure against shuddering damage.

And this is the oncoming truth – a bluff
of foam that no longer hides the roaring
rocks, and a lee shore black as tar;
this, and the pale ship powering on,
buried in a sky-blue sea.

Alfred Wallis's Vision

He saw how the land broke
on the shores of the sea,
how the ocean took on the colours
of the earth, and behind the lighthouse
whose tip seeded the dark
with winking brightness, there was nothing
but dead children.

For the grey sea laid claim
to everything as it shot
up over the shuddering deck,
the waves racing aloft
to soak the grey sails
and muffle the sky in a shawl
of grey salt.

And what was the land worth
but rag-and-bone,
birds in their fidgety kingdoms,
a few red-leafed trees
on a hillside, tiny houses?
And hymns played much too feebly
on an old melodeon.

Under everything lay
nothing from books
or London, but the huge fish
deaf to the world, gliding
on in their languid smoothness,
intent, slower than any
collapsing wave.

Staring at the boats heeled over
in the blue streets of St Ives,
the luggers, schooners, cutters
all alive in the wind and tide,
he saw that *each boat of that fleet
had a soul, a beautiful soul
shaped like a fish.*

A Flourish
(for Jimmy)

What if it were not at all
as painters once thought, the resurrection –
no marble lids flipped up, no smart
unsurprised bodies somehow jerked
back to the vertical?

Suppose it instead an abandonment, almost
casual, in springtime, all the cars
left on the sunlit roads, their doors
wide as open wingcases, engines
quietly ghosting.

Their owners having simply drifted over
to the cowslip kingdom of undropped keys,
into meadows where they kneel at flowers,
or beechwoods where they stroll across thresholds
of light and cover.

Here the orchid rises from the cross,
spilling droplets of blood from its stem,
and beneath the trees unlettered bluebells
wash onwards for ever, leaving the eye
at an utter loss.

Everything merges here – A and O
are as one, from Ophelia's early purples
to Ariel happily listening for owls;
and the little fritillary's chequered shade
is pure art nouveau.

And God? Would hardly, perhaps, believe
how simple his own life had become
on the far side of the trumpets, having
only to budget for continuance and devise
new sports and variations on love.

The Cablecar

The silver box rose lightly up from the valley,
ape-easy, hanging on by its one arm;
in minutes, it had shrunk the town to a diagram,
the leaping river to a sluggish leat of kaolin,
the fletched forests to points it overrode.
It had you in its web of counterweights,
of circles evolved to parallel straight lines.

Riding the long slurs, it whisked you over
the moraine's hopeless rubble. It had your heart
in your mouth at every pylon, where it sagged,
leaned back, swooped on. It had you hear how ice
cracked on the cable. It had you watch it throw
an already crumpled shadow of bent steel
onto the seracs. It made you think of falling.

By the time it lowered you back to the spread valley,
to the broad-roofed houses decorated with lights,
you could think only of what it was like to step
out, at the top, onto the giddy edge
of snowfields still unprinted, that pure blaze;
to be robbed of your breath by the thin air, by a glimpse
of the moon's daytime ghost on solid blue.

Hyphens
(for Helen)

Ice-work

On a moorland walk you stopped
to point to tufts of ice
forced from furrows of wood
along the top of a gate –
brittle seedlings, a crop
planted in the curves of the grain.

A month later, alone
in a city where ice bearded
the hawsers of make-believe steamers
and the wind ached in the marrow
of every secret bone,
I thought of that gate again –
those pressures, expressed as lightly
as the absence of your arm in mine.

One-two

One whose ghost-moth light burns
at the first quarter, filtering down
from the window tall as a ladder propped
at the stair's turn.

Two that ride the hall clock, rising,
falling faces on a starry wheel,
with cheeks pomaded red, and candour
in their brown eyes.

They know nothing of affinity, though
coming or going, they mime the mechanics
of feeling – a shy half-smile, opposite
an eyeful of sorrow.

Out past the window's twenty-four panes
something else, like a wish, like a fact,
is drawing across the darkness, plotting
its graph of gain.

Beyond counting, beyond all harm,
it gathers light and shade to the point
where, cubby-holed, the old moon lies
in the new moon's arms.

Heart-shaped

We may read them as such –
the fountain's bouquet,
the cool landscape
of the painted fan
with its latticed tea-house,
the copious sparks
of red and silver
that shoot from the lips
of a Roman candle,
lavish as spikenard.

We know the subtext –
how the water spills
over stone, and at dusk
the level breeze
moves into the snowdrops.
How the imprint of fire
is seared by darkness.
How even here
in the heavy earth
the heart can blossom.

After-image

Propped on your arms and wearing
a Panama, you stretch out
beside the Loir, at ease
among arrests and arrangements –
the river's solid stillness,
grey-green, dabbed with lily-pads,
the far bank decked with poplars,
a bee glued on the air
at a clump of tressy flowers,
one sandal, pink, discarded,
the light which had been pouring
off your splayed book, your open
smile as you turn to consider
the person taking the picture.

But already the camera's
sharp biopsy is developing
its own after-image:
crushed grass-stems flicking
back into place, some leaves
drifting here and there
onto the drifting river –
a real likeness of absence,
the point of definition
at which, for instance, the poplars
meet the uncertain mist,
and something harder to explain
than light and shadow, more frangible,
becomes your photograph's true frame.

As When
(for Doctor Virendra Bhandari)

As when you gingerly open prayerful hands
to see what you have caught, that has been tickling
your palms with wings or feelers, and you find
only the thought of something bright and precise,
that must have somehow zig-zagged back to the sky,
its image too soon blurred to an idea.

As when, now, I try to recall the delicate
pink of the water hyacinths in Orissa,
the sweep of the beach at Puri, brown beneath
a haze in which stood huge sand-clogged propellers,
or the face of the modest doctor at Udaipur,
or the Konarak boys who wanted their picture taken.

As when they soar, the colonizing words,
up past the rattling crow trapped in the rafters
of San Thomé cathedral, past the pink hives,
humming with breezes, of Jaipur's great façade,
up to the vultures circling Golconda, to claim
a bird's-eye view beyond all contradiction.

As when MacNeice at Sheikhupura, finding
a massacre, did what he could to help the survivors,
but must have had to face again the shadow
that, dark as Durga, stalks his poems, an avatar
of absence cold as the stillness which comes with starlight
to haunt the high hot courts of Fatehpur Sikri.

As when, at evening, gently the descending plane
inclines its wingtip towards the thin blue cloud
that drifts over the city, bringing you back
to what is real, the river with silver burning
in its veins, the earth rich and needful as it is,
a true *swaraj* of absolute instances.

swaraj: self-rule

Slack

After the long etceteras of the flooding tide,
before the surf rattles back through the beach's knucklebones,
the sea's fallow is as still as the twist of milk
which Vermeer's milkmaid tips slowly and for ever
from a jug to a shallow bowl.

The fishing-boats winched to the top of the shore for winter
lie awkwardly stern on to the steely horizon,
stranded in the damp acoustic of an amnesty
declared between past and future, where all storms
approach as smothered thunder.

Calm of a kind – but unnerving, like the serene
gaze of Piero's pregnant madonna, whose hand
resting on her belly must already feel, above
the unbroken waters, the stirrings of a mortal god,
the hard place of the skull.

Like Crossing a Room in the Dark

Something enjoys the thought of a minor challenge
and wants to swim in the dark, among the objects
that live there. It becomes a burglar's game
with rules you make yourself: not to stub
your toe, knock into chairs or tables, or
make a noise. You push off from the door,
stop to guess at shapes – your eyes can do
no better than dark purple. And to listen.
Somewhere a slow clock is lying in wait.

What is it that the room seems to expect?
Why should you think the furniture is swelling
to half its size again? You drift your arms
to feel the air ahead. You say to yourself,
I have a purpose, my own expectations.
I am crossing a room in the dark: foolish enough,
but harmless. On the far side there must be a door.
You breast the night like a dreamer, waiting to strike
the first giant chair, the first boulder of dust.

Threshold

Here nothing is certain, there will be no hour
of arrival, no imperative of departure.

All too often the sun wastes its power
in a blank oblong which slants across the floor.

She looks back from the open door to the bed,
but is she thinking *still*, *not yet* or *already*?

Those petite ankles, the red shoes with their straps –
you feel for her, whatever may not happen.

She waits, in her shiny hat. A train trawls
the misty horizon. The door stands there, yawning.

Familiars

(for Erica)

The relic

In a desk drawer
among loose shuffles
of receipts, old diaries,
chequebook stubs,
photos, strange keys,
it surfaces now
and then – a long
blonde scimitar
of shorn hair
warm to the touch,
not plaited
for a locket or ring
but disgracefully casual,
just lightly bound
with a blue ribbon:
and is somehow shocking,
like finding the sun
adrift for ever
in an endless sky.

A daughter's dream

As the black gale crashed
into the flinching fir-trees
on the hill behind the house
she told me the secret
of her first bad dream:
the eyeball, her own, being sliced
open – she could see it happening –
by a bright searing scalpel.

Enter the triangular facets
of a cut brilliant: her inheritance
of split vision recurring,
of a name under a name.

Sister and brother

When she was small, it was easy for him
to put his higher arm round her
as the early pictures show: and even
the one where he seems to be choking her
in her pram has always been understood
as a show of brotherly affection.

At Pendeen, near the two black foghorns
rearing seaward, they are standing together
in a field, holding hands. That must have been
the last undivided summer. Later,
it is always her with an arm round him.

Subtractions

The family mathematics are simple:
now and again take one away.
One from a set of spoons, leaving five,
One from a family of four: three stay.

The one subtracted has a different name
at different times: great-granny absconding
with milk fever, or a father met
rarely, or a mother there and gone.

One alone in a house with two women,
one alone in a house with two men,
one alone in a hospital bed,
one alone, starting again.

Carried over

That Christmas, she even let me
give her a piggyback, since she was shoeless,
to show her the black atomic berries
of the ivy, its frosted umbels high
up on the wall – and close to them
the sugary white and pink rims
of a single iceberg rose. Thus
she carries me over time's thresholds.

As If

As if borne up on some angelic thermal
to a point from which the body of the earth
explained itself entirely in sunlit distance –
the fields patched with crops, swelling and falling
within their mesh of hedgerows; a peaceable column
of smoke from somewhere stretching upwards, thinning;
the towers and the rubble of cities brought together
as a working map; the fringes of the sea laid
out in white at the foot of the far horizon.

As if you were not still waiting here, at the edge
of a shorn field of fire, for the barrier to lift
and, with luck, for the surly guard to wave you on
past the spindly watchtowers and the freshly turned earth
into another country where you may not settle.

Aftermath

Earth's resistance to the blade,
a second grassy sweetness,
a second wave of summer:
like a trick, a return,
a reward not looked for,
like late sunlight, like a stone
hot to the touch in October,
like the surprise of a love
long ago dismissed
or never sensed till now,
like the cool heart of longing,
like a suddenly simple sky.

And after the aftermath?
No further illusions this year.

Six Songs

Ants

Who are pitiless and certain?
Who carry seed and harvest?
Who are the cemetery workers
whom death only briefly diverts?

Who build tunnels and hills?
Who may be soldiers or thieves?
Who are multiple as molecules,
immortal just by overspill?

Who run in arpeggios, raving
up and down the scales?
Who act in concert, a swarm
of hemidemisemiquavers?

Whose are these frantic feelers,
these shed wings, these defences
for a pale and bloated queen
surrounded by wheeler-dealers?

Who, considering them, could start
to be wise? Or humanly witness
their plural pulse, and not long
for the languid singular heart?

Atlas Cedar

From the soft pad of your ground
you strive skyward, dowsing
the sun in your high darkness,
at night housing whole sheaves
of stars. You stand like a rocket
frozen by a god at the very
second of launch, with the casing
split halfway up into four,
and all the fuel and vapours
spilt into solid splays
of branches and starburst clusters
of needles that flare their green.

And still it is the heavens
that you aim for: if you dream,
it would be of Titanic power
enough to rip your roots clear
of the dark, and send the tether
of ivy falling slowly
back from your trunk as you rise.
As you rise, and your rough bark
straightens to smooth metal.
As you rise and shake off the earth,
at one with the sun's gold fire,
the white fire of the moon.

Little Owl

It may be that the little owl
has drifted into my dreams at owl-light.

It may be that I have half seen
the turn of its wing, in a low swoop
as it dips and rises close to the ground.

It may be that the little owl
has held my stare in its own, by the road
where sometimes it sits on the tall post
or a pile of books, bobbing, bobbing.

And all of this may be half forgotten –
but never that call which rises from a steady
forlorn morse to a frayed edge
of fear, of anger rising, urgent.

Across the fretted parkland it carries
beyond all doubt, scouring the grass
with rage and its sobbing coda of regret.

Into my heart it sinks like a claw,
into the dark from which nothing escapes.

Stag Beetle

For three or four months it has got a life
and is testing it here – a miracle toy
that is all contraption, a Swiss army knife
in mid-air with all its gadgets deployed.

The antlers shine, the wing-covers gleam,
the wings vibrate – the whole device
shakes with effort, alarming as a dream
no flight engineer would wish to have twice.

Precise as a Fabergé egg, it is whirling
through the summer dusk, cruising for a fight:
later, after it has got its girl,
it will sup at the oak tree's sappy delights.

It lumbers, it zigzags, it banks and veers,
tacking up to the crowns of the trees –
ungainly, yet able to commandeer
the fickle angles of the evening breeze.

In the wake of its whirring, something stays
like the ghost of a smile, imprinting the air
with an echo that outflanks the passing days
and lays time's clockwork contrivances bare.

Grey Heron

Mantled in yourself, you believe
every whisper and chuckle
of the river. You stand for hours,
patient as a priest, allowing
the water to wrap itself
again and again round your legs.
Here each movement is measured –
a foot delicately lifted
and shaken and slowly lowered:
or the bill that blitzes the surface
in a flash to stab at a fish.

Later, under your wings'
calm beat, you traverse
a land of sunlit fields
held down by a net of hedges,
with puffs of parsley forests
and little streams that glint
silver as any fish.
Languidly your feet trail
across the sky. You believe
every shifting current
in the broad reaches of the air.

Lime Trees

Beyond, the full moon has cast
its pallor onto the park,
onto the liminal levels
that ride in a simmer of light.

But here, under the lime trees,
all heights and depths are warded
by the heart-shaped, saw-toothed leaves.

The roaring July bees
have gone, heavy with nectar,
and the night breeze hardly stirs
any last fragrance of flowers.

And here, under the lime trees,
the air is alert for the least
shift of a leaf or a wingbone.

What so intently seethes
in the echoing colonnade
is a spell, or something you know
but cannot quite make out.

And under the lime trees that block
the moon, there is only the jag
of your heart beating, beating.

Sloes

No lack of present wonders –
the rowan's star-showers
stopped with blood,
the polished ochre
of acorns, some
clamped in their cups,
or the pungent sapwood
locked into each tight bead of holly.

But the darkest amazements of all
in the bright scour
of autumn riches
are the sloes that hang
among wicked spines,
their blue-black skin
misted with a bloom
like breath staying on a flawless mirror.

Cutting one open, you find
a simple pulp
of greeny yellow,
weak moonlight,
and a single nubble
bedded in blister-water,
a bone-hard core,
an oubliette that beggars belief.

From somewhere, the purest birdsong –
last flarings
of the cherished light.
Always you return
to the sloe, to test
the coinage, to conjure
from its sour heart
the future perfect of its white flowers.

Estuarial

(for Kevin and Linda)

Cormorant and heron preside
over shiny flanks of sleech.
Sky becomes more and more
of an issue. Light promotes
itself in oystery silver,
pink and grey.

Out in the open at last,
away from that green darkness
of upstream, that waltzing drift
of madness, where bluebells blurred
everything and the salmon leapt
rigid into air.

And not yet swept out past
the land's faltering goodbyes
of chevroned huts, a frayed
red flag, to the first
tufts of spray, the great hoop
of the homeless horizon.

Boats nod at their moorings.
Trains come and go
blindly, huge and leaning
on their curves. Low walls
hold back the onlooking shores
where silence is a settlement.

Here, too, there are still
secret transactions – between
the last of fresh water
and the inroading tides; or
summer heat and the constant
burning of the heart.

An Organic Recital

Even before we reached the Impromptu by Vierne,
in fact during the Prelude and Fugue in E Flat
by Bach (J.S.) – the key, it is thought, representing
the Trinity, as might also the three main subjects
of both prelude and fugue – my heart started
its tricks, its random *fugato* of racing flurries.

I thought of the echocardiogram, its absurd
pictures – of, for instance, the mitral valve with its flap
of something that could have been skin or stretched gum
and which lifted, wavered about and somehow flopped
back into place. I already had my own picture
of the atrium, all that blood pouring in from the veins.

Meanwhile, however, in the windchest the stickers opened
and closed the pallets on orders transmitted by
the backfalls and trackers. Draw-stops moved the sliders.
The swell-box waggled its Venetian shutters, the couplers
linked pedals with great. While the flue pipes thundered,
the reeds continued to flutter their metal tongues.

Such hidden systems, such faith in synchronism!
And all this even before we reached the Impromptu
by Vierne. Impromptu – literally, on the spur
of the moment. Louis Vierne, the French composer
and organist who, blind from birth, died
in the middle of playing the organ in Notre Dame.

Out of Time

One moment, caught in the circle
with hints of the prism at its edges,
the striped lighthouse and, beyond it,
a sedate yacht that dips
in sunlight against a perfectly
curving horizon: the next,
the whole view guillotined
by a black disc.

One moment, the red rattling
into the two hundred,
the white played off the cushion
to glide into the hundred
and both of them rolling back:
the next, the table no longer
ticking, the balls trapped,
thudding on the bar.

One moment, the currency convertible
to anything, it seems: the next,
it is no longer an issue
except as the small change
weighing on your eyes.

For Jon Silkin

The flowers of your poems persist –
and each must answer to its name,
its own nature: dandelion,
a bluebell, lilies of the valley,
peonies, the strawberry plant,
a daisy, crowfoot in water,
the violet, milkmaids, moss,
goat's-beard and daisy, harebell.

They will not be bound as a garland
or pinched to a wreath: it is
their natural wealth which carries
your voice. Under your lodestar
with its pointed demands – to be exact,
yet various; to judge, yet to love;
to wander, yet believe in home –
they bud and blossom endlessly.

Kaddish

This is a song of a song gone missing
in which children were fearless and ran
straight for the eye of the wobbly camera,
put out their tongues and waved their hands.

This is also the raw edge of music
the black intervals' virtual dissonance
in which the violin almost remembers
how once it played for weddings and dances.

In the missing song, grown-ups were kind
and parents there to run into, always –
mother in the dress that smelt of safety,
father taking pictures of family holidays.

Here is the way back never to be taken
to the peaceable kingdom of praise and thanks
where all puffs of gunsmoke simply exploded
into lightsome feathers, and all bullets were blanks.

This is a song of a song gone missing,
with words simple as pebbles, inferring
a sense that the mind can no longer admit
or the heart still quite unlearn.

Allotments in Winter

The plots shrink in their drenched sorrows to a scrawl
of husks and hanks, the blackened heads of sunflowers,
with a small flourish of ice-plant here or there,
some bushes dotted with a few berries:
like the sketchy outlines of a story which could in time
acquire the status of a minor classic, whose ending
might be uncertain, but would still give some credence
to delight and the word fleshed in detail –
the ribbing of the wheelbarrow's tyre printed onto mud,
the clang of the spade striking a spark from stone,
the poplars' last highlights that wave all day
from a sky scoured to brightness for tomorrow.

3

Out of Silence

It is the silence of the world that is real
THOMAS MERTON

Beneath the civic gardens and the roots
of plants, under the blue fumes,
the darkness at first reports nothing
to displace the world above,
or its cold air nipped by the cries of finches.

But change follows change: the threshold turns
to a corridor, then to a room filled
with a morse of footsteps tapping overhead,
then comes the rush of a drowning downpour,
resolved as a pool where every ripple
converges to drain away at the centre,
leaving only the red earth. The water
brought to nothing, and with it
the flesh and all its working parts.

Yet here, in the starless sump of the city,
the siren songs of its weathered people
are held on stems of silence that prove
unbreakable: black frequencies
that fill and empty, fill again.

*

Nibbana – the cooling of the fire, the calming of the wind, the settled
quality and sensitivity of still water
VENERABLE SUCITTO BHIKKU

The wind gets up slyly – flicks a bud,
tests a twig, the dip of a branch,
dies away to nothing and begins again.

In its middle period it edges down
chimneys, puffing dark soot into rooms,
twangs wires, volleys some birds over hedges,
dies away to nothing and begins again.

Until it roars in the high fir trees,
rams the isobars together, knocks
ships into rattling cupboards, the waves
into furious slopes of marble whipped with spindrift.

Until it slackens for a few moments,
releases its grip on the hunched cyclist,
removes its support from the figure leaning
into it, then buffets them both back to the strain.

Until, sooner or later, it collapses
and the blossom no longer trembles, its petals
as if already fallen to the cloud-bright water.

*

Don't forget Valentine's Day
NOTICE SUSPENDED IN SUPERMARKET

Goodbye hope to see you again soon
All night the unspoken words
track across the screens
of the checkouts – all retail romances
demand that goodbye is hello,
that shopping is what goes on
happily ever after
hope to see you

All is well, beneath
the unblinking harvest lights –
the meats are covered with paper,
the shelves restocked, thousands
of gleaming bottles rub shoulders,
plenty walks down the aisles
see you again

Here all noise has been channelled
into ducts, or the phlegmy dozing
of constant refrigeration,
here is the world in a chain
of brands, of air-freighted seasons,
each place a clone of everywhere
again soon

You must not think that gorse
is out of bloom, that anyone
is sobbing in a corner, afraid
that kissing is out of season,
or that something has been forgotten
though endlessly repeated
soon goodbye hope
Goodbye hope to see you again soon

*

Oh silence, independent of a stopped ear,
You observe birds, flying, sing with wings instead
DAVID WRIGHT

All these stories are waiting
in the mind, on the tip of the tongue,
to be told with the precious lips
and the true language of the hands:

how the leaves failed in their rustling
and the birdsong died away
taking conversation with it;

how later, cars stopped even
purring, and pneumatic drills
were pure vibration that crazed
the tarmac and quaked the flesh;

how planes would come unstuck
without a sound, lifting
to beg the simple air;

how, last of all, a rocket
rose from a cushion of flame,
its wake a billow of brightness
and the sky, a great blue ear
into which the silence spiralled.

*

*The name of Oradour indicates that from the Roman period there was
there an altar and a place to offer prayers for the dead... Alas, it could
never have better deserved the name it received*
GUIDE TO ORADOUR

No silence less elected than these –
the silence of the tailor's sewing-machine
the silence of the garage workshop
the silence of the rasping trams
the silence of the hotel cutlery
the silence of the burnt church
the silence of the cleaver
on the butcher's board
the silence of the school
Oradour

The silence of the ladle
in the silver tureen
the silence of watches stopped
at the last time of day
the silence of passbooks
the silence of family photos
the silence shut into barns
the silence of witnessing silence
the silence we carry in our blood
Oradour

*

There, where the long street roars, hath been
The stillness of the central sea
TENNYSON

Duck-egg or cobalt, pillars of cloud,
mackerel, mare's tails, a field of open blue –
away from the flare of mustard pitched on the cliff,
the sky takes out its options on the view.

The sea has its own work to do, lifting
the swell, and handing boats from here to there –
or magnifying raindrops to pools that bubble
as if all the fish in the world were sipping the air.

And once in a blue moon, the horizon
vanishes, leaving the boats to struggle, snared
like black insects in a dove-grey mesh: and the sun
a pearl set in silence, the sea and the sky's blank stare.

*

Even if you don't win you can't lose
BINGO HALL PROMOTIONAL OFFER

This is the shape which outdoes word or number,
the shadow free of desire and regret,
but not the round face of alarm or wonder,
not the sun rising or the moon setting,
not the alpha, not the omega,
not a halo or a spangled dome,
but the O of your dreams, a thought balloon
circular as a reel of film projecting
the life to be lived for ever, and soon,
round as a cannonball breaching the ring
of everyday worries, round as a bubble
that rises, shining, clear of trouble:
the O in fortune you watch as it tracks
your progress. From the basket your own face stares back.

*

Great Streets of Silence led away
To Neighborhoods of Pause
EMILY DICKINSON

Outside, the noise of traffic like a clean sweep:
here, the tick of wood, the cobwebbed window,
the dew-lipped flowers, the bulrush of the bellrope.
Air slack in the organ-pipes: Gabriel leaning
across to Mary, across the golden arrowheads
of morning light. Something is always waiting
to be disclosed, to be received, that cannot
be rushed or delayed, that has to find its moment.

Till then, the candles still not budding into flame,
the authority of the atmosphere barely challenged,
the joyous dove still kept from hurtling earthward,
the slightest of breezes wafting the hanging fringes
of the altar-cloth. All day, the traffic outside.
The traverse of sunlight. The least echo worked on
by silence, by the faithful worm of silence.

*

I will make you brooches and toys for your delight
of bird-song at morning and star-shine at night
ROBERT LOUIS STEVENSON

Moonfire catching each crystal in the rock,
silence attracting attention to itself,
stones measuring the knowledge they lack –
when the blurry fleece of mist lifted off,
every feature was made an example:
the stars, the corroding frost, even
the amber-eyed flock of milling sheep
which passed through deepest moon-shadow as if
dumbstruck, without any hope of bleating.

Further east, between the shoulders
of the hills I, too, was dazzled by darkness,
eyes bruised by staring, with only
the fraught river to take at its word.
And what were words to make of the stars,

so many and flagrant, green, white, red,
that burst through so suddenly, cloud-clearing?

Only later, when the dawn dipped down
into the valley, came the sense of a song –
one intimated but not yet begun,
the blank pages of a notebook lying
open, rinsed in a fervour of light.
Slowly the landscape started to advance,
at first still wearing the green and black
of night-time. And then the birds began,
their high songs plentiful as the stars.

*

You cannot solder an Abyss
With Air
EMILY DICKINSON

As if in a dream, the chestnut trees
fall away, their turrets shrinking.
Below, threading the early mist,
birds reduced to tiny floaters
bathe in the great ocean of the air.

You would not need to be a god
to love a planet captured like this –
the sweet logic of the fields etched
with the plough's cursor, racetracks, cities,
each in its place; a hum of traffic
on miles of good roads; a dog barking;
and every fault a feature of sense.

What holds is a balance struck between
the roar of the frayed uplifting flame
and the drift of silence, that pear-drop shadow
which swells and darkens with each inch of fall
back to the solid, hollow ground beneath.

The Enclosures

Four unexpected meadow flowers slide out from
the sky-blue letter you sent from Kyrgyzstan –
a clover with pink bristles, a blue vetch
faded to light mauve, a yellow crucifer,
a white chickweed. They lie here, tiny, flattened,
intact – as delicate as any of the wreaths
found buried with the ithyphallic boy-king
and all his rubble of riches: the collarette
with little love-apples and berries of woody nightshade
strung on strips of palm; or the farewell garland
of olive leaves, blue water-lily petals
and cornflowers, which someone left on the dark threshold.
    These, too, paling with absence, recast love's spell
    as open pathos, and time as immortelles.

Lawrence Sail was born in London in 1942 and brought up in the west country. A freelance writer, he has published eight collections of poems, most recently *Out of Land: New & Selected Poems* (1992), *Building into Air* (1995) and *The World Returning* (2002), all from Bloodaxe Books. He has compiled and edited a number of anthologies, including *First and Always: Poems for Great Ormond Street Children's Hospital* (Faber & Faber, 1988) and (with Kevin Crossley-Holland) *The New Exeter Book of Riddles* (Enitharmon, 1999). His poems have been broadcast on radio and television, and he also written a radio play. He reviews for *Poetry Review* and contributes a regular column to *PN Review*.

He was editor of *South West Review* from 1981 to 1985, chairman of the Arvon Foundation from 1990 to 1994, director of the Cheltenham Festival of Literature in 1991 and co-director in 1999. He was awarded a Hawthornden Fellowship in 1992 and an Arts Council writer's bursary the following year. In 1991 he was a Whitbread Book of the Year judge; from 1994 to 1996 he was on the jury of the European Literature Prize. He has frequently worked abroad for the British Council, including visits to India, Egypt, Bosnia and Ukraine. He is a Fellow of the Royal Society of Literature.